Gift of Place

Gift of Place

Margaretta Mitchell

Calligraphy by
Georgianna Greenwood

The Scrimshaw Press

©The Scrimshaw Press 1969
Library of Congress
Catalog Card Number 76~84197

Published at Berkeley
The Scrimshaw Press
Publication number 3
P.O. Box 9192
Berkeley, California 94709

Design by Margaretta Mitchell
Offset Lithography by
Cardinal Company of San Francisco

The Scrimshaw Press emphasizes the
work of previously unpublished artists.
Publications will usually be in limited
edition, with the artist working closely
with the editors on design, layout
and production.

" But the eyes are blind.
One must look with the heart...."

ANTOINE DE SAINT ~ EXUPÉRY

In the special places of our lives
we live those relationships most
dear to us. There in those secret
corners, we discover ourselves;
we take our places in the greatest
of all creations.

These images are events from the
childhood which surrounds me.
I know that image cannot match reality,
but it can become an offering
from memory to Life,
one person to another,
me-you, eye level.

I offer this book-for me, for you,
for the child who unites our spirit-
because it should be enough
to share the joy of being alive.

For Nell
a garden bouquet
remembering September afternoons
and May mornings.

There was a moment once—
when my children were very young
one a baby still, sweet flesh,
the other not yet a wise four years.

There was a time, then,
when the Earth was mine.
I felt life boldly within,
harmonious without.
Everything was in its place.

Living in that enclosed circle of new life,
I saw the first paintings of childhood
    from the windows of the house
Gathered the rare jewels of childhood
    in shells and stones from the sea,
Heard the music of childhood
    in rustling leaves on canyon paths
    beneath the live-oaks;
Felt the freedom of childhood
    in the dancing, leaping bare bodies
    on hot summer days.

And knew that peace children find
in the words of evening stories
ending in dreams.

In the rush of days, the crowd of tasks
that pushes us further from ourselves,
Where is space for life?

If I could give you only one gift, Child,
now, in my love,
Take this gift of Place.

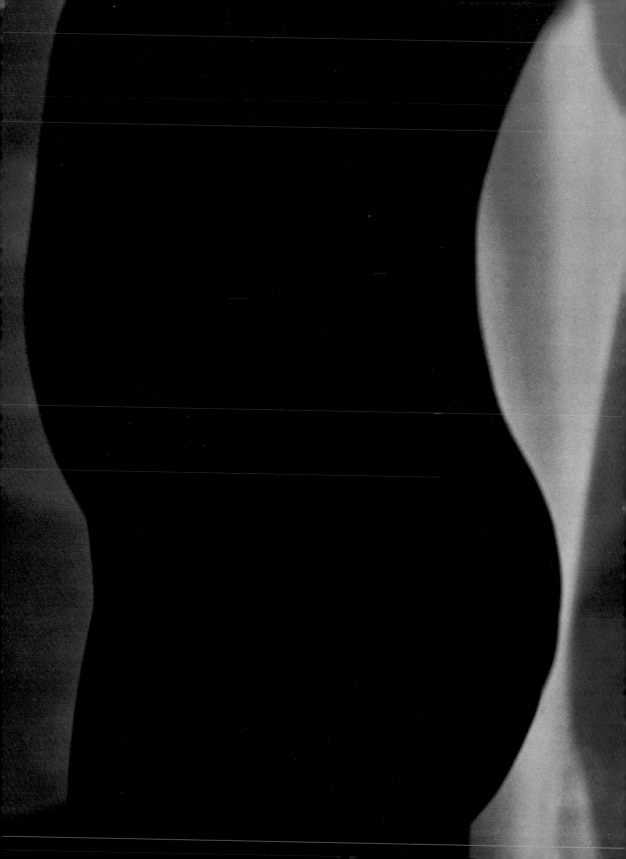

Give, woman, give
to the head-strong, plunging world
your sense of self.

Do not tire of talking from your heart
trust it.
It is your great gift:
your place.

But how can you know that?

From depths, call for heights
Draw up the children into taller selves.
Give will to man that he may know himself.
Lead from mind to heart, from heart to soul.

Do not lose the ancient trust,
the sacred meanings.

Love, woman,
sustain Life.

They say
the saints
awoke each morning
to a new day
found fresh
the air,
were reborn
in the morning sun.

I say
that children
live a world
each day

As those saints knew
they know
how
to love the world they find.

Leave the child in us
that in the morning
of maturity
we may be
reborn.

'I like it here,' she says
'Home's my best.'

At four years
what does she know of
places, palaces, or princesses?
Everything!

They live in her windows
dancing in the reflected light.

She is the princess
This place is her palace.

'How do you build a palace?'
she asks me.

Eyes we have, but do we see?
We recognize the familiar
without seeing beyond
into the grey-mist mornings,
the bright, blue-shadowed afternoons,
the long silver-fogged evenings.

The familiar house stands
on a wooded hillside
facing the bay
defying time.
Wisteria branches
gnarled and twisted
frame the balcony.

Not an ancient house, but California-old;
great hearted, it held the secret
which became this book.

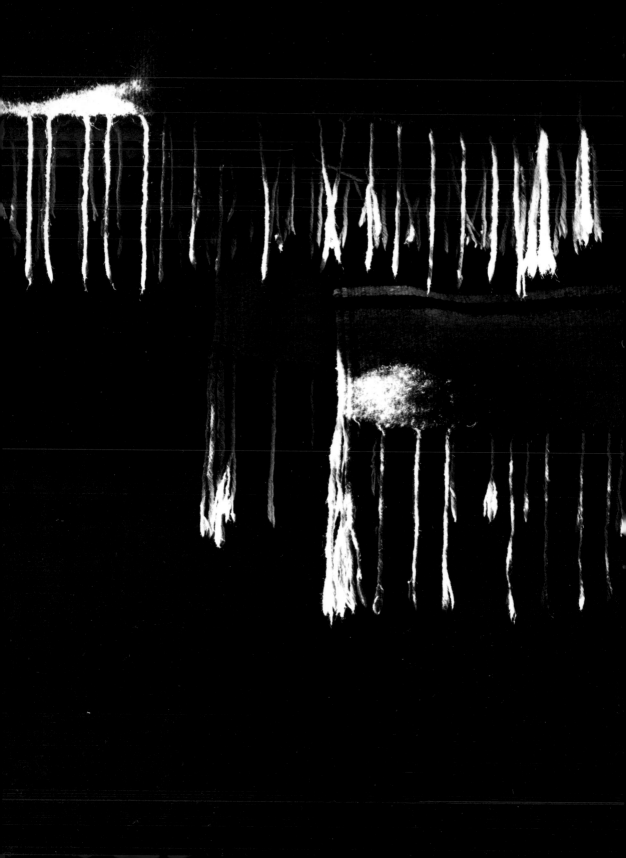

Come, be
Come, play

Forget what you have learned
Leave the cluttered desk.

Find your world
with my map.

Go directly to the heart

There
ask nothing
take all

Come with me,
a child.

I am a poet
only if all children are poets.
Nothing is taught, only learned
those who learn, teach.
You understand
I mean no formal school —
Life.

Poet-child
create my house
environment
Family.

The breath is Love.
The gift is Place.

Home of childhood —

Reality comes soon enough
outside the door.

I build the walls strong
bolt the door.
Shall I take the key along?
(the crooked-toothed one?)

Yes, for homecomings.

Tender greetings & gratitude
to those friends and family who appear
in these pages as follows:
Arlyn, Edward,
Sarah, Tersh, Anne, Peter, Deidre, Frederick,
Kate, Janvrin, Frederic, Margaret, Ben, Susan,
Laura, Stephanie, Andrea, Antea.

Special Thanks
to my Mother and Father for their trust,
to Nell Dorr for her unique sense of beauty,
to Dave Bohn for his disciplined eye
to Frederick for his love

Let not my thanks to thee—
rob my silence—
of its fuller homage.

RABINDRANATH TAGORE